SCIENCE EVERYWHERE!

Healthy Eating

The Best Start in Science

By Helen Orme

NEW
FOREST
PRESS

First published in North America in 2010 by New Forest Press,
PO Box 784, Mankato, MN 56002
www.newforestpress.com

TickTock project editor: Rob Cave
TickTock project designer: Trudi Webb

ISBN 978-1-84898-289-5
Library of Congress Control Number: 2010925467
Tracking number: nfp0002

Printed in the USA
9 8 7 6 5 4 3 2 1

Picture credits (t=top, b=bottom, c=center, l=left, r=right,
OFC=outside front cover, OBC=outside back cover):

iStock: 9tl, 14br, 18t. Shutterstock: OFC all, 1 all, 2, 3 all, 4-5 all, 6-7 all,
8 all, 9tr, 9b, 10-11 all, 12-13 all, 14tl, 14bl, 14-15, 15 all, 16-17 all,
18b, 18-19b, 19 all, 20 all, 24 all, OBC all.

Every effort has been made to trace the copyright holders and we apologize in
advance for any unintentional omissions. We would be pleased to insert the
appropriate acknowledgments in any subsequent edition of this publication.

Contents

Any words appearing in the text in bold, **like this**,
are explained in the Glossary.

Food tastes good and
it can be fun to eat.
But why is food good
for our bodies?

Fruit   Pasta   Vegetables

Food makes us feel better
when we are hungry.

Eating a **balanced diet**
with lots of different foods
will give your body all the
nutrients that it needs.

What's so good about bread?

Bread is a **carbohydrate** food.

So are pasta, rice, cereal, crackers, and potatoes.

These foods give you long-lasting **energy**. They help you run and play without getting tired right away.

They also give you **fiber** which helps your **digestive system** work smoothly.

Jacket Potato

Carbohydrate treats include popcorn, your favorite sandwich, or a baked potato.

Sandwiches can have lots of different fillings.

7

What's so good about vegetables?

Vegetables like lettuce, and cucumber, are real super-foods.

Salad

They all have important **vitamins** and **minerals** that your body needs.

Vitamin A, helps your eyes to see better in the dark.

B Vitamins help your body turn food into energy.

The mineral potassium, found in peas and cucumbers, helps your muscles work.

Vegetables also have fiber to help your digestive system.

Vegetable pizzas and soup are great ways to enjoy vegetables.

What's so good about fruit?

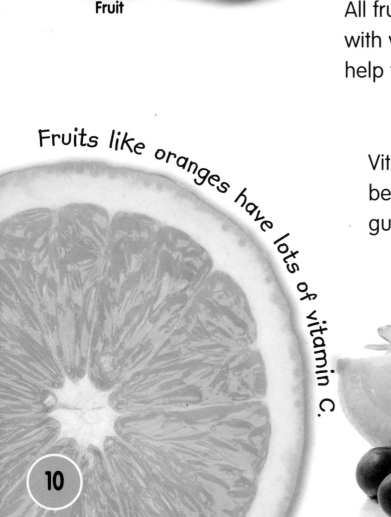

Fruit

All fruits are packed
with vitamins that
help to keep you well.

Fruits like oranges have lots of vitamin C.

Vitamin C is important
because it keeps your
gums healthy.

Vitamin C helps your body's defenses keep you well—fighting **infections** and diseases.

Fruit kabobs are a fun way to fill up on fruit.

Fruit kabob

You should try to eat at least five **portions** of fruit and vegetables every day.

What's so good about meat?

Meat—like meatballs, turkey, chicken, lamb chops, and steak—has lots of **protein**.

Meatballs

So do fish, eggs, baked beans, and nuts.

Your body uses protein to make new muscle and skin **cells**.

Some delicious ways of eating protein are eggs, hot dogs, fish fingers, and hamburgers.

All these foods also have **iron** to make your blood healthy.

What's so good about milk?

Dairy products like yogurt, ice cream, and cheese are all made from milk. Dairy products all contain calcium.

Milk

Milk is something your body loves.

Calcium is an important mineral that helps make the bones inside your body strong.

Calcium keeps your teeth strong too.

A delicious way to get your calcium is yogurt with fruit.

Yogurt

Milkshakes are a good source of calcium.

Milkshake

What's so good about butter?

Butter and margarine have lots of **fat**.

Butter

We all need some of the fat in butter, margarine, and vegetable oils.

Fat helps you to absorb some of the vitamins from the other foods you eat.

Oil

But too much fat is bad for you.

16

There are other foods that have lots of fat.

Cookies

It's OK to have candy, cookies, and chips— as a treat!

But remember to leave room for all the good things your body needs.

And remember to brush your teeth at least twice a day to keep them healthy!

Chocolate

17

What's so good about water?

Your body is made up of lots of water.

If you weigh 40 pounds (18 kilos), 26 pounds (12 kilos) of that is water!

But your body keeps losing some of that water.

Exercise that makes you sweat, going to the bathroom, even just breathing—all of these make you lose water.

Your body tells you that you've lost a lot of water by making you thirsty.

You can get some water by eating fruits and vegetables with lots of water in them, like grapes and melons.

You should drink 6-8 glasses of fluids every day!

19

Where does my food go?

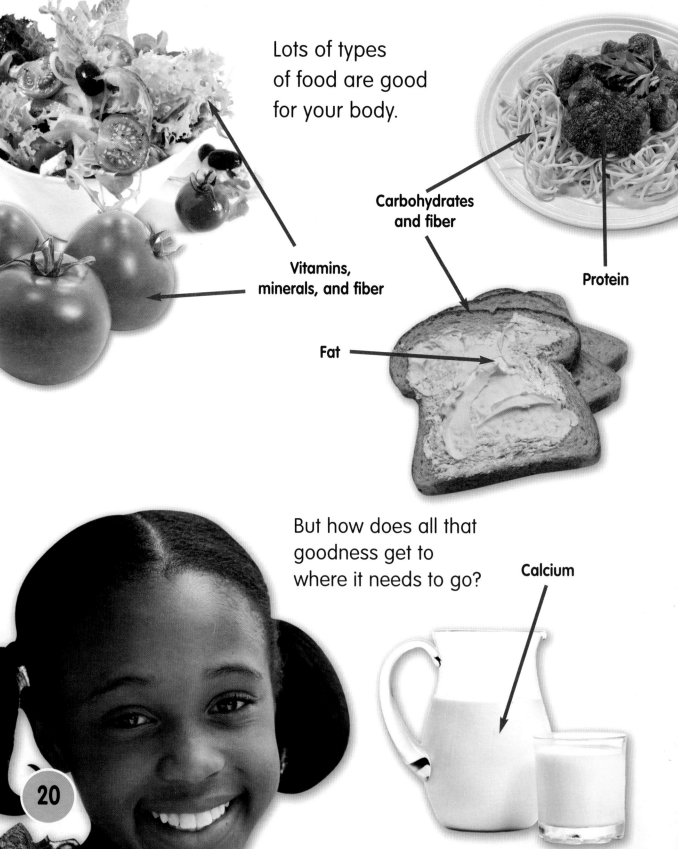

Lots of types of food are good for your body.

Carbohydrates and fiber

Vitamins, minerals, and fiber

Protein

Fat

But how does all that goodness get to where it needs to go?

Calcium

The answer is digestion—the way your food gets broken down so your body can use it.

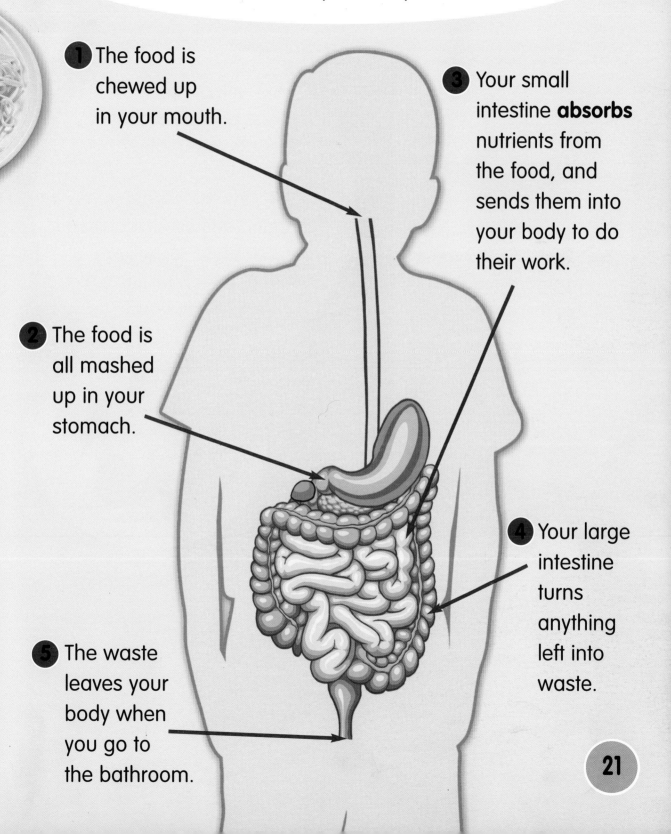

1 The food is chewed up in your mouth.

2 The food is all mashed up in your stomach.

3 Your small intestine **absorbs** nutrients from the food, and sends them into your body to do their work.

4 Your large intestine turns anything left into waste.

5 The waste leaves your body when you go to the bathroom.

Questions and answers

Q Which is the most important meal of the day?

A Breakfast is the most important meal of the day.

Q What counts as one portion of fruit and vegetables?

A One tablespoon of chopped fruit or vegetables; or one piece of fruit; or a small glass of fruit juice; or one tablespoon of dried fruit.

Q What vitamin can be found in oranges?

A Oranges contain lots of vitamin C.

Q Which "fruit" is really a vegetable?

A Rhubarb is actually a vegetable.

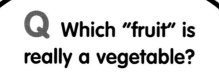

Q What animals do we get milk from?

A We get milk from cows, goats, and sheep.

Q What are people called who don't eat meat or fish?

A They are called vegetarians.

Q Which fruit or vegetable contains the most water?

A A cucumber contains the most water.

Q How many teaspoons of sugar can be found in a normal bar of chocolate (two ounces/60 grams)?

A There are seven teaspoons of sugar in a normal bar of chocolate.

Glossary

Absorb To take something in so it can be used.

Balanced diet Meals and snacks that include foods from all the food groups in the right amounts.

Calcium A mineral that helps make bones and teeth strong.

Carbohydrate An important nutrient the body uses for energy.

Cells The smallest building blocks of living things. Your body is made of cells.

Dairy products Milk and foods made from milk.

Digestive system All the parts of your body that take part in digestion.

Energy The ability to be active and do things.

Fat A nutrient that provides energy, and helps your body absorb some vitamins.

Fiber A kind of carbohydrate that helps your digestive system.

Fluids Anything you can drink.

Infections Illnesses caused by germs.

Iron A mineral found in meat, spinach, dried beans, apricots, and some other foods. It helps make your blood healthy.

Minerals Special substances that come from water, soil and rocks, and cannot be made by living things. We get minerals from plants which take them in from water and soil, and from animals that eat plants.

Nutrients The goodness in food which your body needs to grow and to work properly.

Portions The amount of any food that you eat at one time.

Protein A nutrient that helps your body make new cells and repair old ones. It is needed for growth.

Saliva The liquid made in your mouth which starts the digestion of your food.

Vitamins Special substances found in tiny amounts in our food. They help our bodies turn the food we eat into energy to keep the body healthy.

Index